BENSON & HEDGES proudly presents
another in a series of volumes dedicated to
good taste · · ·

ENTERTAINING WITH STYLE
a collection of recipes from great American
restaurants.

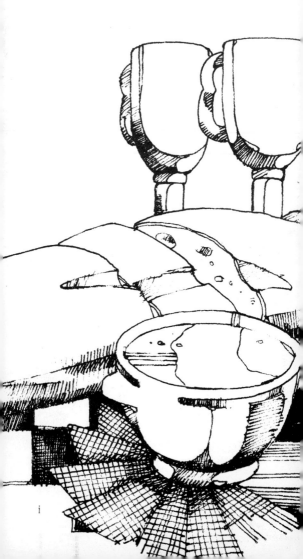

ii

Photography by William K. Sladcik
Food styling by Fran Paulson
Produced by Meredith Publishing Services

The food photography and menus in this book are designed to provide ideas for serving the recipes in your home and do not necessarily represent the way the dishes are served in the various restaurants.

Published by
Philip Morris Incorporated
for Benson & Hedges
100 Park Avenue
New York, New York 10017

Printed in the United States of America.

Foreword

ENTERTAINING WITH STYLE is a collection of creative ideas for entertaining at home. Benson & Hedges has asked 32 of America's great restaurants to contribute a favorite recipe, and added menu suggestions to help make your next party a success.

The featured restaurants span the country, bringing you a taste of the world's great cuisines. You will find French, Italian, and Japanese delicacies, plus some of this country's delightful regional food specialties. All have helped their restaurants become hallmarks for good food and stylish dining.

Whether you are planning a formal dinner for eight, a quiet late-night supper for two, or a casual picnic for four, the menus have been carefully designed to help make that event unique. Also, hints are included to help you prepare the menu selections at home. A separate section gives recipes for a number of popular appetizers.

ENTERTAINING WITH STYLE has ideas to enhance a variety of occasions. So, the next time you get together with good friends, enjoy the party — Benson & Hedges style.

Contents

Locke-Ober
Café

Locke-Ober Café

Boston, Massachusetts

More than 100 years ago, two restaurants sat side by side in an alley just a block from the Boston Common. One was named Locke's; the other, Ober's Restaurant Parisien. But as most Bostonians came to know, the drinks were better at Locke's, the food at Ober's. So naturally everyone raised a glass at Locke's, then walked next door to dine. Fortunately for the culinary arts, the wall separating the two was removed in the 1890's and the Locke-Ober Café was born — and began to thrive.

Today much of the Victorian elegance remains — carved mahogany woodwork, lavish chandeliers, and brass-studded leather. Old and treasured recipes are the hallmark of the Locke-Ober. One mainstay from earlier years, Breast of Chicken Sauté Richmond, is still served under glass with characteristic Boston elegance.

Breast of Chicken Sauté Richmond also makes an outstanding entrée for contemporary dining at home. Because the "main event" is prepared in two separate stages, you can easily divide your time between the kitchen and your guests.

A CONTEMPORARY AMERICAN DINNER

Oysters on the Half Shell
Breast of Chicken Sauté Richmond*
Wild Rice   Green Salad
Strawberry Shortcake   Coffee
Wine: California Riesling

BREAST OF CHICKEN SAUTÉ RICHMOND

- 4 chicken breasts, boned
- 6 tablespoons butter
- 12 medium fresh mushroom caps
- ¾ cup dry sherry
- ¾ cup light cream
- 4 ¼-inch-thick cooked ham slices
  Cream Sauce
  Salt
  Pepper
- 4 slices white bread, toasted

In a large ovenproof skillet sauté chicken, skin side down, in *3 tablespoons* of the butter until golden brown. Turn chicken over and add mushrooms; cook 5 minutes longer. Pour off excess drippings. Add *half* of the sherry, *half* of the cream, the ham slices, Cream Sauce, and salt and pepper to taste. Cover and bake in a 350° oven for 30 minutes or till chicken is tender.

Quarter toast diagonally and place in each of 4 individual skillets or au gratin dishes. Place a slice of ham over each and top with a chicken breast and a few mushrooms. Add remaining butter, sherry, and cream to sauce in skillet; blend well with a wire whisk and cook 2 to 3 minutes over medium heat. Strain sauce and pour over chicken. Cover each dish with foil; bake in a 400° oven for 10 minutes. Garnish with *parsley,* if desired. Makes 4 servings.

Cream Sauce: Melt ¼ cup *butter* in saucepan over low heat. Blend in ¼ cup *all-purpose flour,* ½ teaspoon *salt,* and a dash *white pepper.* Add 1¾ cups *light cream* all at once. Cook and stir over medium-high heat till mixture thickens and bubbles. Makes 2 cups.

Hint:
Wild rice is a truly American food. It is the seed of a grass which grows wild in the northern United States, and is expensive because of the difficulty of harvesting. Enjoy the flavor and texture of wild rice and keep the cost down by combining cooked wild rice with an equal amount of cooked white or brown rice.

Windows
on the World

Windows
on the World

New York, New York

From the 107th floor of the World Trade Center, a glistening New York is served up for your viewing pleasure. For your very special dining pleasure, Windows on the World serves its patrons delights for both the eye and the palate. In fact, you have your choice of three intriguing eating spots: The Hors d'Oeuvrerie, The Cellar in the Sky, and The Restaurant.

At the Hors d'Oeuvrerie you can choose from dozens of internationally renowned appetizers prepared by chefs in colorful native dress, or simply relax with afternoon tea, sandwiches, and pastries. The Cellar in the Sky is a lovely restaurant within a restaurant. Here dining is limited to 36 epicures an evening who are treated to a 7-course meal designed around 5 wines chosen by Chef Henri Boubee and Cellarmaster Kevin Zraly.

From the tiered rows of tables in The Restaurant the view is unequaled — up to 50 miles on a clear day. The tempting menu reflects the world that seems to lie within view — from Scandinavian Steak Sauté to Scallopine of Veal with Wild Mushrooms.

At your next party, bring a little of this globe-trotting cuisine to your home by serving one of The Restaurant's great desserts — Frozen Soufflé Amaretto. The beauty of this almond liqueur-flavored macaroon mousse is that it's made ahead and frozen so it can be served at a minute's notice. Keep it on hand for spur-of-the-moment entertaining.

AN INSTANT PARTY

Frozen Soufflé Amaretto*
Liqueurs and Cordials
Fresh-brewed Coffee

FROZEN SOUFFLÉ AMARETTO

- 4 macaroon cookies (⅓ of an 8-ounce package)
- 6 egg yolks
- 2 eggs
- ¾ cup granulated sugar
- ¼ cup Amaretto liqueur
- 2 cups whipping cream, whipped
  Additional whipped cream
  Additional crushed macaroons

Crumble macaroon cookies into coarse pieces. Spread crumbled macaroons in shallow baking pan and dry in 300° oven for 20 minutes, stirring once. Cool. Makes 1 cup crumbs.

In a large bowl combine egg yolks, whole eggs, and sugar; beat on high speed of electric mixer till thick and fluffy, and sugar is dissolved, about 6 minutes. Continue beating, gradually adding liqueur. By hand, fold in whipped cream and ¾ cup of macaroon crumbs. Prepare six 6- or 8-ounce individual soufflé dishes with 1-inch buttered aluminum foil collars or a 1-quart soufflé dish with a 2½-inch buttered aluminum foil collar. Gently spoon soufflé into dishes and freeze at least 4 to 6 hours. To serve, top with additional whipped cream and sprinkle with remaining macaroon crumbs. For prolonged storage, wrap frozen soufflé in aluminum foil or seal in airtight containers. Makes 6 servings.

Hint:
Make the coffee you serve as special as your soufflé. Visit a local specialty store and buy a sampling of exotic coffee beans — Hawaiian Kona, French roast, Mocha Java — there are many to choose from. Use a grinder or a blender to grind the coffee beans fresh as you need them.

The Russian
Tea Room

The Russian Tea Room

New York, New York

What began over 50 years ago as a meeting place for transplanted Russian émigrés has grown into a must-visit restaurant for patrons from around the world. The legendary Russian Tea Room on New York's west side is a spot where old-world cuisine and traditions remain constant.

The menu at The Russian Tea Room reflects the diversity of the vast Russian landscape. For example, Shashlik Caucasian, among the Tea Room's most notable entrées, originated in the colorful Caucasus region of Russia and has been a staple meal of the natives for over 3,000 years. A variation of shish kebab, the dish consists of a few basic elements: marinated leg of spring lamb on a skewer with tomatoes, onions, and green peppers broiled over a bed of wood embers or charcoal.

You can easily re-create this dish in your kitchen, or have some fun and cook it outdoors as has been done for centuries in Russia.

DINNER À LA RUSSE

Cold Borscht with Sour Cream
Shashlik Caucasian*
Bulgur Wheat
Russian Beet Salad   Black Bread
Strawberries Romanoff   Coffee
Wine: Pinot Noir

SHASHLIK CAUCASIAN

- 2 pounds boneless lamb, cut into 2-inch cubes
- 1 cup cooking oil
- 2 teaspoons lemon juice
- 1 teaspoon salt
- 1 teaspoon pepper
- 1 bay leaf
- 1 teaspoon dillweed
- 1 small clove garlic, minced
  Tops of 4 stalks of celery, coarsely chopped (1 cup)
- 3 tomatoes, quartered
- 2 onions, cut in wedges
- 2 green peppers, cut in squares

Place lamb in large bowl or shallow dish. In screw-top jar combine oil, lemon juice, salt, pepper, bay leaf, dill, garlic, and celery; pour over lamb. Cover and marinate in refrigerator for 6 to 8 hours or overnight, stirring occasionally. On each of 4 long skewers, thread lamb, tomato, onion, and green pepper; repeat, using 4 to 5 cubes of lamb on each skewer. Grill shashlik over medium coals 12 to 16 minutes, turning once. (Or, place shashlik on rack in shallow baking pan, 4 inches from broiler. Broil 10 minutes, turning once, for medium rare.) Brush meat and vegetables with additional marinade, if desired. Serve on a bed of hot cooked *rice*. If desired, garnish with *fresh dill*. Makes 4 servings.

Hint:
To properly grill the shashlik, line up hot coals in parallel rows in the firebox as well as around the edge of the grill. Stagger the skewers on the grate directly above the spaces between the charcoal rows so meat fats will not drip on the coals, causing flare-ups.

The
Coach House

The Coach House

New York, New York

When you enter The Coach House Restaurant, you're struck with its understated elegance — high ceilings, brick walls, 19th-century paintings, intimate tables, and gentle lighting. The Coach House has been called a true "American" restaurant — one where old-fashioned American and delicate continental cuisines are offered side by side. Here, hearty chicken pie, baked Idaho potatoes, and southern pecan pie are proudly served alongside Mignonettes of Veal à la Campagne with Glazed Chestnuts, Chicken Sec Sautéed with Fresh Mushrooms, and Dacquoise, a crunchy hazel-nut meringue torte. And no matter which meal you choose, a crunchy corn breadstick accompanies it for a distinctive Yankee touch.

One Coach House appetizer that blends well with any entrée is fresh Mushrooms à la Grecque, a very easy and versatile dish that can be served anywhere in style. Take these herbed, marinated mushrooms on a picnic, or serve them at a crystal and candlelight dinner.

AN APPETIZER SUPPER

Fresh Mushrooms à la Grecque*
Bacon-wrapped Chicken Livers
Tater Peels with Parmesan
Fresh Vegetables with Spinach Dip
Cheese and Fruit Platter
Fried Zucchini and Cauliflower
Selection of Wines

15

MUSHROOMS À LA GRECQUE

- 2 pounds fresh whole mushrooms
- 2 cups water
- 1½ cups dry white wine
- ½ cup olive oil
  Juice of 2 lemons
- 2 large onions, sliced
- 2 bay leaves
- 1 teaspoon whole peppercorns
- 2 unpeeled cloves garlic, washed and crushed
- 4 sprigs Italian parsley
- 1 stalk celery, coarsely chopped
- 2 teaspoons salt
- 1 teaspoon oregano
- 1½ tablespoons finely chopped fresh parsley
- 1 tablespoon finely chopped fresh dill
- 1 teaspoon crushed black pepper

Wash mushrooms well and set aside. In a 4-quart Dutch oven combine water, wine, olive oil, lemon juice, onion, bay leaves, peppercorns, garlic, parsley sprigs, celery, salt, and oregano. Bring mixture to a boil and add mushrooms; cover and boil for 8 to 10 minutes. Remove mushrooms from broth and place in a deep bowl. Continue boiling broth 15 minutes longer; strain broth and discard vegetables. Cool. Quarter large mushrooms and add cooled broth. Sprinkle with chopped parsley, dill, and crushed pepper; marinate in refrigerator for several hours before serving. Makes 4 servings.

Hint:
Be sure to dry mushrooms thoroughly after washing. The caps tend to be more tender than the stems. If you wish to use only the caps, turn each mushroom on its side and cut the stem so some remains in the cap — this way the cap will hold its shape. Use the stems in a sauce or casserole.

The Palm

The Palm

New York, New York

From its beginnings as a speakeasy during the rousing days of Prohibition, The Palm Restaurant has been regarded by New Yorkers as the best steak house anywhere — a place where generous portions and a relaxing atmosphere are the norm. Owners Bruce Bozzi and Walter J. Ganzi, Jr., grandsons of the founders, have retained the charm of the early days. Floors are still covered with sawdust, and their grandfathers' three-point rule is still in effect: buy the best, cook it faultlessly, and serve it swiftly. At The Palm there are no menus. Instead, each waiter recites the day's menu: "Fried shrimp, fried scallops, baked bass, roast lamb ..." Just stop him when you hear what you want!

Steak is The Palm Restaurant's premier entrée. One such dish that's a true beefeater's delight is Steak à la Stone, a sliced filet mignon sautéed with pimiento and onion and served over toast points. In keeping with their reputation, the standard portion served at The Palm is a hefty one pound of prime beef per diner! At home, however, you can plan on two or three servings per pound, so this recipe makes enough for a party of 8 to 10.

A BEEFEATER'S DINNER AT HOME

Tomato Bisque
Steak à la Stone*   Caesar Salad
Cheesecake   Coffee
Wine: Zinfandel

STEAK À LA STONE

4 pounds beef filet mignon, cut 1½ inches thick

4 large Spanish onions, sliced and cut in strips

1 cup butter, melted

4 4-ounce jars pimiento, cut in strips
  Salt
  Pepper
  Toast points

Place meat on cold rack of broiler pan. Broil 3 inches from heat to desired doneness, turning once. (Allow 14 to 16 minutes total time for rare; 18 to 20 for medium.) Meanwhile, in a large skillet sauté onion in butter till tender; add pimiento and salt and pepper to taste. Cook and stir mixture for 2 to 3 minutes. Cut broiled steak in thin slices; add to sauce. Serve immediately with toast points. Makes 8 to 10 servings.

Hint:

Tomato bouillon, a delicious alternative to Tomato Bisque, can be easily prepared. Combine 1· 10½-ounce can of condensed tomato soup, 1 10½-ounce can of condensed beef broth, half a soup can of water, a dash of garlic powder, and a dash of crushed oregano. Bring to a boil and simmer 5 minutes. Serve in warmed bowls and top with thin avocado slices or a spoonful of sour cream.

Frog

Frog

Philadelphia, Pennsylvania

Since 1973 a storefront restaurant — unpretentiously named Frog — has become a leader in Philadelphia's restaurant renaissance. A pleasant, youthful ambience fills the place. Along with the excellent food, Frog is proud of its 150-label wine list and features a special "wine of the day" served by the glass, in addition to the regular house wine. In this way, diners are able to try new wines without buying an entire bottle.

The eclectic menu at Frog is utterly imaginative and changes frequently. Many of the dishes are a delicious blend of French and Thai influences. The combination is credited to the Thai employees who first worked in Frog's kitchen.

The French and Thai influences are very apparent in the Frog recipe for Thai Chicken Curry. The sweet, pungent sauce is made with a French béchamel base spiced with far-eastern curry. Thai curries are generally hotter than East Indian curries, but this westernized version is a bit milder. Create an authentic flavor with curry paste, already subtly seasoned with fish and coconut milk. Look for canned curry paste at Oriental food markets.

A CURRY ADVENTURE FOR TWO

Shrimp Soup

Thai Chicken Curry*   Rice

Puris

Coconut Cream Pudding with Mango Sauce

Tea

Wine: Gewürztraminer

THAI CHICKEN CURRY

- 2 tablespoons corn oil
- 2 teaspoons curry paste
- 12 ounces boned skinless chicken breasts, cut in ¼-inch strips
- 2 tablespoons sugar
- 2 tablespoons soy sauce
- ¼ teaspoon salt
- ¼ teaspoon minced garlic
  Béchamel Sauce
- 1 cup broccoli flowerets, blanched 1 minute and drained
- ¼ cup salted peanuts
  Hot cooked rice

Heat oil in large skillet or wok over low heat. Add curry paste and cook for 1 minute, stirring to combine oil and curry. Turn heat to medium-high and add chicken, sugar, soy sauce, salt, and garlic. Stir-fry till chicken is done. Stir in Béchamel. Add broccoli and peanuts and cook just till heated through. Serve with rice. Makes 2 servings.

Béchamel Sauce: Melt 2 tablespoons *butter* in saucepan over low heat. Blend in 2 tablespoons *all-purpose flour*, ¼ teaspoon *salt,* and a dash *white pepper.* Add 1 cup *milk* all at once. Cook and stir over medium-high heat till mixture thickens and bubbles. Cook 1 minute more.

Hint:
The traditional pan for stir-fry cooking is the wok. When using a wok, position the ring stand on the largest burner of your range. For a gas range, place the ring wide end down; for an electric range, place the ring wide end up. Electric woks are available, too, and are great for at-the-table cooking.

Chesapeake
Restaurant

Chesapeake Restaurant

Baltimore, Maryland

The very mention of this 75-year-old seafood restaurant makes your mouth water for the delectable bounty of Chesapeake Bay. How do you like your oysters — raw, fried, or Baltimore style? Whatever your choice, you'll find it here. Or you may decide to order fresh steamed clams direct from the Bay. If crab is your weakness, choose from Maryland crab cakes, stone crab, crab fingers, mushrooms stuffed with crab, or Crab Imperial Chesapeake.

For a delicious taste of the Maryland coast no matter where you live, you can prepare Crab Imperial Chesapeake at home. Serve it hot or chilled — whichever best suits your party plans. In fact, you can prepare the entrée early in the day, chill it, then bake the filled crab shells once the guests arrive. For a delicious cold meal, prepare the filled shells entirely in advance and serve them chilled on a bed of fresh lettuce.

AN EASY ELEGANT DINNER

Cold Leek Soup
Crab Imperial Chesapeake*
Breadsticks   Spinach Salad
Lemon Chiffon Pie
Wine: Mosel Riesling

CRAB IMPERIAL CHESAPEAKE

- **1 green pepper, finely chopped**
- **2 pimientos, finely chopped**
- **2 eggs**
- **1 cup mayonnaise**
- **1 tablespoon salt**
- **1 tablespoon English mustard**
- **½ teaspoon white pepper**
- **3 pounds lump crab meat**
  Additional mayonnaise
  Paprika

In a bowl combine green pepper, pimiento, eggs, the 1 cup mayonnaise, salt, mustard, and pepper; mix well. Add crab meat and mix gently, being careful not to break up crab pieces. Spoon mixture into 8 crab shells or individual casseroles, mounding lightly. Spread tops with a thin layer of additional mayonnaise and sprinkle with paprika. Bake in a 350° oven for 15 to 18 minutes. Serve hot, or chill and serve on a bed of *lettuce*. If desired, garnish with *lemon* and *tomato rose*. Makes 8 servings.

Hint:
To prepare crab shells for stuffing, select large perfect shells and scrub them thoroughly with a wire brush. Place the shells in a Dutch oven and cover with hot water. Add 1 teaspoon of baking soda and bring to a boil. Simmer, covered, for about 20 minutes. Then drain, wash, and dry the shells. This removes the fishy odor. The shells may be stored and re-used. Just simmer again with baking soda after each use.

The
Big Cheese

The Big Cheese

Washington, D.C.

A restaurant that specializes in tasty cheese dishes is such a great idea, it's a wonder that someone didn't open one long ago. Barbara Witt, owner and founder of The Big Cheese, believed that the nation's capital needed a fresh approach to restaurant food. She settled on cheese as an economical food ingredient with a universal appeal.

Given the variety of nationalities in the Washington area, the cheese theme also allows for much menu experimentation. In fact, Barbara changes the menus every two months.

Three special favorites on the menu are Trekokker, a Norwegian Camembert fritter in a beer batter; Fritto Misto, a delicate Italian mixed fry of Bel Paese, mozzarella, and fresh vegetables; and Pohani Sir, a Yugoslavian cheese specialty.

Pohani Sir is everything a fine Swiss "raclette" is, and then some. Delectable Gruyère cheese is covered with a crumb coating, deep-fried, and served with a savory mayonnaise.

A CHEESE SUPPER

Pohani Sir*
Boiled New Potatoes with Parsley   Pickles
Fresh Fruit Cup
Wine: Yugoslavian Riesling

POHANI SIR

  1 **pint cherry tomatoes, halved**
  1 **tablespoon butter, melted**
 12 **ounces Gruyère cheese**
  1 **cup fine dry bread crumbs**
  3 **tablespoons all-purpose flour**
  2 **eggs, well beaten**
    Cooking oil for deep-fat frying
    Pohani Mayonnaise

In a skillet sauté tomatoes in butter for 1 to 2
minutes; set aside. Cut cheese into ½-inch-thick
squares about 4x4 inches; cut each square
diagonally to form 2 triangles. Combine bread
crumbs and flour. Dip cheese triangles into
beaten egg, then into bread crumb mixture; let
stand a few minutes to dry. Dip cheese in egg,
then in crumbs again; chill to set coating. Heat
oil to 375°. Fry cheese quickly until golden
brown, about 1 to 2 minutes; drain on paper
toweling. Garnish cheese with sautéed
tomatoes and serve with Pohani Mayonnaise.
Makes 4 to 6 servings.

  Pohani Mayonnaise: In a small mixer bowl
combine 1 tablespoon *Dijon mustard,* 1 tablespoon *white vinegar,* ½ teaspoon *Worcestershire sauce ,* ¼ teaspoon *salt,* ¼ teaspoon *white
pepper,* 2 dashes *hot pepper sauce,* and 2 *egg
yolks.* Beat at medium speed till blended. At
high speed add ½ cup *salad oil* 1 teaspoon at a
time. While continuing to beat at high speed,
add 1 cup *salad oil* in a thin steady stream till
well blended, scraping sides of bowl
occasionally. Makes 1⅔ cups.

Hint:
For a different slant on this delicious recipe,
have several types of cheese available, such as
Fontina, Jarlsberg, zesty Cheddar, or hard
cheeses of your choice. Cut and bread the
cheese ahead of time and refrigerate it. At cooking time, offer each cheese on a separate plate
and fry the cheese to order.

Csikós

Csikós

Washington, D.C.

Csikós owner-chef Rainer Thuleweit and his wife, Etzsebet, have succeeded in bringing a bit of their native Hungary to Washington, D.C. The city is much the richer for it.

Paprika, or "Turkish pepper," is a dominant seasoning in Csikós Hungarian cooking. As you might expect, of the more than 30 entrées featured, many proudly incorporate this robust red spice. The unmistakable flavor, piquant aroma, and rich color of paprika add a special zing to all it touches. But take a tip from the natives: paprika should be used sparingly — just enough to enhance, but not cloud, the other food flavors.

If you'd like to try this delicious spice at its tastiest, try Csikós' recipe for Rabbit Paprikas. The rabbit pieces are simmered in a sauce of red wine, paprika, onion, green pepper, and tomato. Just before serving, sour cream, another ingredient favored by Hungarian cooks, is added.

A HEARTY HUNGARIAN DINNER

Rabbit Paprikas*   Spaetzle
Green Salad
Hungarian Pancakes with Jam and
Whipped Cream
Coffee
Wine: Châteauneuf-du-Pape

RABBIT PAPRIKAS

¾ cup chopped onion
3 slices bacon, chopped
1 tablespoon cooking oil
2 rabbits, cut up
1 large green pepper, chopped
1 large tomato, chopped
2 cloves garlic, minced
1 tablespoon sweet Hungarian paprika

continued

35

    1½ teaspoons salt
    ¼ teaspoon white pepper
    1 cup red wine
    ½ cup water
    1 cup dairy sour cream
    ¼ cup all-purpose flour
    ¼ cup water
       Spaetzle

In Dutch oven cook onion and bacon in oil till
golden. Add rabbit, green pepper, tomato, garlic, paprika, salt, pepper, wine, and the ½ cup
water. Cover and cook till rabbit is tender, about
45 to 60 minutes. Remove rabbit and keep
warm. Strain gravy and measure juices. Return
juices to Dutch oven and boil until reduced to 2
cups. Reduce heat to simmer. Meanwhile,
blend sour cream, flour, and the ¼ cup water;
add to juices and cook and stir till thickened.
Return rabbit and heat through. Serve with
Spaetzle. Makes 4 to 6 servings.

   Spaetzle: In mixing bowl stir together 2 cups
all-purpose flour and 1 teaspoon *salt*. Add 2
slightly beaten *eggs* and 1 cup *milk;* beat well.
Place mixture in a coarse-sieved colander. Hold
over large kettle of rapidly boiling salted water.
With wooden spoon, press batter through colander. Cook and stir 5 minutes; drain
thoroughly. Makes about 3 cups.

Hint:
Most of the paprika found on supermarket
spice shelves is of the Spanish type. Imported
Hungarian paprika, which gives an authentic,
more pungent flavor to the dish, can often be
found in specialty and gourmet shops.

Casa Grisanti

Casa Grisanti

Louisville, Kentucky

Louisville's Casa Grisanti was built by three generations of Grisanti family restaurant expertise. Over the years, this popular dining spot has successfully made the transition from a basic menu of spaghetti and pizza to one that features a complete range of flavorful northern Italian cuisine. Today, Casa Grisanti is a romantic establishment filled with candlelight, green plants, and fresh flowers. Dramatic tableside preparations are a common sight throughout the dining room. Casa Grisanti features milk-fed veal, scampi Verona-style, rack of lamb with mint and garlic, as well as a variety of lighter pasta specialties.

Pesto, a unique sauce that originated in Genoa, is an essential item in any restaurant that caters to northern Italian cuisine, and Casa Grisanti is no exception. Their delicious recipe for Fettuccine con Pesto is a great choice for at-home entertaining. The sauce's rich green hue comes from the use of fresh basil leaves, making it a popular seasonal dish that can be enjoyed all summer long. At Casa Grisanti, the recipe is featured as a classic first course, but this delicate dish can serve as an entrée as well.

A FETTUCCINE SUPPER

Prosciutto and Melon
Fettuccine con Pesto*
Lettuce and Artichoke Salad
Espresso   Italian Pastries
Wine: Frascati or Chenin Blanc

FETTUCCINE CON PESTO

1 cup fresh basil leaves
¾ cup olive oil
¼ cup grated Parmesan cheese
1 tablespoon pine nuts
1 teaspoon minced garlic
½ teaspoon salt
¼ teaspoon freshly ground pepper
12 ounces fettuccine

In a blender container or food processor combine basil, olive oil, cheese, pine nuts, garlic, salt, and pepper. Process till smooth.

Cook fettuccine in 6 to 8 quarts of boiling salted water, stirring occasionally to prevent sticking. Cook pasta till al dente or "tender to the tooth," about 3 to 4 minutes. Drain pasta, reserving 2 tablespoons of the salted water. Add the 2 tablespoons reserved water to the pesto sauce; stir to blend. Toss pesto with hot fettuccine. Makes 6 servings.

Hint:
Although fresh basil, a key ingredient in pesto sauce, is available only in the summer, you can enjoy Fettuccine con Pesto throughout the year. Prepare a big batch of the pesto sauce with fresh basil and freeze in one-meal quantities for winter dining. Be sure to bring the frozen sauce to room temperature and stir it well before tossing with the fettuccine.

Gene & Gabe's
Lodge

Gene and Gabe's Lodge

Roswell, Georgia

Some of our country's most charming new restaurants are housed in buildings more than a century old. Today in Roswell, Georgia, an 1850-vintage Masonic Hall serves as a lovely country dining spot specializing in northern Italian and continental cuisine. Hungry Atlantans regularly make the 25-mile trip for a taste of Gene and Gabe's menu specialties.

One popular dish well worth the drive is Vitello Bolognese, or Veal Bolognese, a blend of veal, prosciutto ham, mozzarella cheese, and Marsala-flavored sauce, topped with fresh mushrooms. You can assemble and cook this superb dish in less than 30 minutes. All you need to do in advance is pound the veal and slice the mushrooms.

AN ITALIAN DINNER

Antipasto
Veal Bolognese*
Rice with Green Peas   Sautéed Zucchini
Fruit Bowl   Espresso
Aperitif: Veridicchio
Wine: Barbaresco or Nebbiolo d'Alba

VEAL BOLOGNESE

- 1¼ pounds veal round steak *or* veal leg sirloin steak
- 2 eggs, beaten
- ¼ cup Parmesan cheese
- ¼ teaspoon salt
- ¼ teaspoon pepper
- 1 cup soft bread crumbs
- 6 tablespoons butter
- 6 slices prosciutto ham
- 6 slices mozzarella cheese
- ½ pound (3 cups) fresh mushrooms, sliced
- 1 cup chicken stock
- ½ cup dry Marsala wine
- 2 tablespoons chopped parsley

Cut veal into 6 pieces; pound to ¼-inch thickness. In bowl combine eggs, Parmesan cheese, salt, and pepper. Dip veal lightly in egg mixture, then in bread crumbs. In large skillet sauté veal in butter for 3 minutes on each side. Top each piece of veal with a slice of prosciutto and a slice of mozzarella cheese. Place veal in baking dish, reserving butter in skillet. Bake in 350° oven about 5 minutes or till cheese melts.

Meanwhile sauté mushrooms in reserved butter. Add additional 1 tablespoon *butter,* if necessary. Add stock and wine. Bring to boil and boil 5 to 10 minutes to reduce to thin sauce. Pour sauce over veal and sprinkle with parsley. Makes 6 servings.

Hint:
Marsala, used in preparing Veal Bolognese, is a Sicilian wine resembling sherry. It is fortified with brandy to bring its alcohol content to about 20 percent. Although Marsala comes in three types — dry, sweet, or semi-sweet — choose dry Marsala for cooking purposes. The sweet varieties can come flavored with almond, making them pleasing after-dinner drinks.

Bern's
Steak House

Bern's Steak House

Tampa, Florida

Steak houses may abound, but the care and creativity that go into everything from the special ingredients, to the unique menu, to the friendly service, rank Bern's among the finest restaurants. Bern's ages their own beef, cuts it to your order, then trims it of all fat before cooking to your exact specifications. Many of the fresh vegetables served are grown on Bern's own farm. And the glamorous ice cream desserts are made with homemade ice cream.

Bern's Brazilian Snow, for one, is a light and lovely finish for a great steak dinner. It is so simple to fix that you can dazzle friends and family with it on the spur of the moment. Just keep on hand a supply of creamy-rich vanilla ice cream and fresh coffee beans. At serving time, grind the beans very fine and sprinkle over the ice cream as you scoop it out of the carton. Each scoop then becomes part velvety ice cream, part robust coffee — the perfect match.

A GREAT STEAK DINNER

French Onion Soup
Broiled Ribeye Steaks with Sautéed Mushrooms
Fresh Garden Greens
Brazilian Snow*   Coffee
Wine: Beaujolais

BRAZILIAN SNOW

⅓ cup fresh roasted coffee beans
1 quart French vanilla ice cream, slightly softened
  Whipped cream
4 maraschino cherries

No more than 5 minutes before serving, grind coffee beans as finely as possible in a nut grinder. Reserve 1 tablespoon of ground coffee. Sprinkle one-third of remaining coffee over ice cream in carton. With an ice cream scoop, scoop out one layer of ice cream and place in serving dishes, mixing coffee and ice cream together as much as possible without over-handling ice cream. Repeat twice more with remaining two-thirds of ground coffee and ice cream. Top each serving with whipped cream and sprinkle with a little of the reserved ground coffee. Garnish with cherries and serve immediately. Makes 4 servings.

Hint:
Serve this refreshing layered dessert in parfait glasses, attractive glass coffee mugs, stemmed goblets, small glass vases, or brandy snifters. If you like, top off each serving with a few whole roasted coffee beans instead of the cherry garnish.

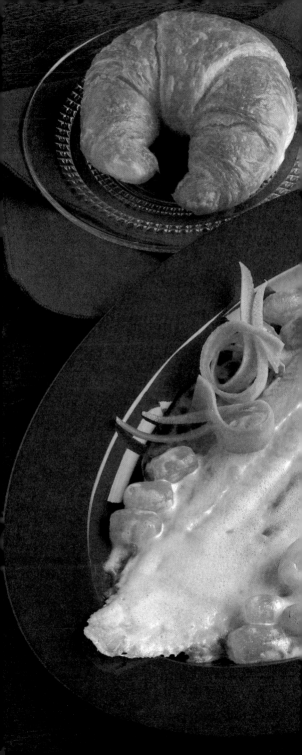

Cafe
Chauveron

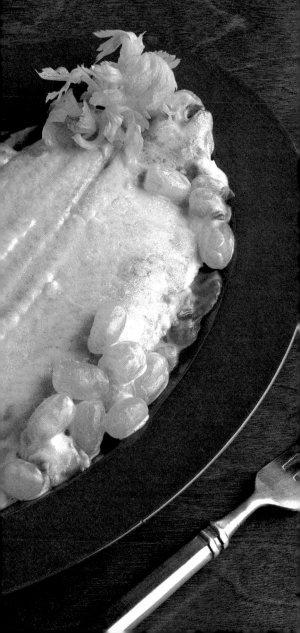

Cafe Chauveron

Miami, Florida

The decor of Miami's Cafe Chauveron resembles the dining room of a stately ocean liner. Like a magnificent ship, the restaurant offers a spectacular view of sea and sky through its thirty-foot window wall. Customers find it easy to imagine themselves aboard a luxurious cruise ship as they dine on delightful French specialties. Cafe Chauveron's extensive menu lists 35 superb entrées, including filet mignon with goose liver and truffle sauce,and roast quail flamed with cognac. The fish and seafood dishes are also extravagant temptations — Maine lobster grilled with snail butter, and bouillabaisse Marseilles-style.

One such elegant entrée is the Cafe's recipe for Sole Véronique. "Véronique" refers to a classic French style of cooking using seedless white or green grapes. Legend has it that a famous French chef had decided to add small white grapes to a delicate wine sauce for a new fish recipe. The wife of one of his under-chefs gave birth to a baby girl the day the dish was premiered, so to celebrate, the chef allowed the dish to be named after the girl — Veronique.

Today, Sole Véronique can be the perfect beginning to a celebration of your own. The fish takes only 30 minutes to cook. Then grapes are placed around the fish, the cream sauce is poured on top, and the feast is placed under the broiler until browned. It is a great way to introduce friends to classic French cooking.

A CLASSIC FRENCH DINNER

Cream of Watercress Soup
Bibb Lettuce with Vinaigrette
Sole Véronique*
Ratatouille   Buttered Rice
Chocolate Mousse
Wine: Brut Champagne

SOLE VÉRONIQUE

- 4 1¼-pound sole
- 1 teaspoon salt
  Pepper
- 2 tablespoons butter
- 4 shallots, chopped
- 3 cups dry white wine
  Cream Sauce
- ¼ cup whipped cream
- 1 cup skinned seedless green grapes

Sprinkle fish with the salt and pepper; place in a large skillet with butter, shallots, and wine. Bring to a boil and reduce heat. Cover and cook 20 to 30 minutes. Remove fish to a heat-proof serving dish. Keep warm. Continue cooking liquid in skillet on high heat, uncovered, till reduced to about ½ cup. Remove from heat and, if desired, strain. Add to Cream Sauce and check seasoning. Fold in whipped cream. Place grapes around fish and pour sauce over all. Place under broiler until browned, about 2 minutes. Makes 4 servings.

Cream Sauce: Melt 2 tablespoons *butter* in saucepan over low heat. Blend in 1 tablespoon *all-purpose flour* and ⅛ teaspoon *salt*. Add ½ cup *light cream* all at once. Cook over medium-high heat, stirring constantly, till mixture thickens and bubbles.

Hint:
Genuine sole is not a native American fish, and fine restaurants must import their supplies. But good substitutes are available in this country, including pompano, flounder, perch, or small trout. Frozen fillets can be used when making Sole Véronique at home.

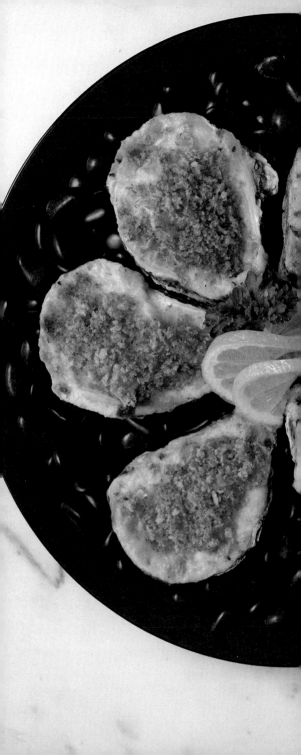

Jonathan

Jonathan

New Orleans, Louisiana

The era of Art Deco glamour has been re-created in New Orleans on the edge of the famous French Quarter. Architect-owner Jack Cosner transformed two 150-year-old town houses into a restaurant showplace that takes its patrons back to the glittery twenties and thirties. To supplement his own extensive Art Deco collection, Cosner used works by two popular artists of the period, Erte and Icart. In addition, contemporary artist Dennis Abbe created elaborate murals on canvas and in glass for Jonathan's interior.

Besides the decorating delights at Jonathan, Chef Tom Cowman caters to the palate as well. His ingenious mix of Creole and continental cuisines deserves the raves of many satisfied gourmets.

Oysters Thomas is one such dish. It features oysters baked on the half shell with crab meat and topped with a medley of intriguing sauces. Serve Oysters Thomas as an appetizer or a fancy main dish.

A NEW ORLEANS BRUNCH

Bloody Marys
Oysters Thomas*
Eggs Sardou
Fresh Fruit Cup   Coffee
Wine: California Chardonnay

OYSTERS THOMAS

- **16** large fresh oysters
  Rock salt
  Béarnaise Sauce
- **1** pound lump crab meat
  Cream Sauce
- **¼** cup dry bread crumbs
  Paprika
  Lemon quarters
  Parsley sprigs

continued

Remove oysters from shells. Scrub half of shells and place on a bed of rock salt in a large flat pan. Put 1 to 2 teaspoons Béarnaise Sauce in each shell; top with an oyster and 1 tablespoon crab meat. Combine remaining Béarnaise Sauce with Cream Sauce and spoon on top. Sprinkle with bread crumbs and paprika. Bake in a 400° oven for 15 minutes or till sauce starts to brown and bubble. Serve with lemon and parsley. Makes 4 servings.

Béarnaise Sauce: In a large skillet combine 1 cup *water*, ½ cup *white wine*, ¼ cup *tarragon vinegar*, 3 finely chopped *shallots*, ¼ cup chopped *onion*, 1 tablespoon dried *tarragon*, and ½ teaspoon coarsely ground *black pepper*. Boil gently, stirring occasionally, till mixture is reduced to ⅓ cup paste, about 30 minutes. Spoon into blender container and process till smooth, adding more wine if needed. Reserve 1 tablespoon; store remaining sauce base in refrigerator for another time.

Place 3 *egg yolks* in a bowl over hot (not boiling) water; beat with a wire whisk till triple in volume, about 5 minutes. Slowly add 1 cup melted and cooled *butter*, beating constantly. Add the 1 tablespoon reserved *sauce base* and 1½ teaspoons *lemon juice*; mix well. Season to taste with *salt* and dash of *cayenne*. Remove from heat.

Cream Sauce: In top of a double boiler combine 2 tablespoons melted *butter* and 2 tablespoons *all-purpose flour*; blend well. Add 1½ cups *light cream*, 1 tablespoon *dry sherry*, a pinch of powdered *thyme*, and *salt* and *white pepper* to taste; place over boiling water and cook for 15 minutes, stirring constantly. Add a small amount of hot mixture to 2 beaten *egg yolks*, then return to hot mixture. Cook and stir 1 to 2 minutes longer.

Hint:
To open an oyster, use an oyster knife or other sturdy, blunt-tipped knife. Insert the knife blade between the shells at the joint of the thick end and twist open; then run the knife blade under the oyster to cut the muscle that holds the shells together.

Brennan's

Brennan's

New Orleans, Louisiana

Great jazz and great food are New Orleans traditions, and so is Brennan's, which first opened its doors on Bourbon Street in the 1940's. Brennan's, now located on Royal Street, is an institution, and "breakfast at Brennan's" is an absolute must for visitors to the city. It is here that a typical New Orleans breakfast begins with an appropriate "eye opener" such as Milk Punch or a Bloody Mary, proceeds to Eggs Hussarde, and ends on a blazing note with Bananas Foster — the flaming dessert that was invented at Brennan's. The food is outstanding and so is the atmosphere — wrought-iron grillwork, beautiful dining rooms, and a lovely courtyard.

While breakfast is special, any meal at Brennan's is a unique experience. The lunchtime crowd also flocks to Brennan's, and Trout Kottwitz is a popular entrée. The delicately flavored fish is cooked with mushrooms and artichokes and served with a buttery sauce. Serve it in the relaxed atmosphere of your own patio or porch and pamper your guests in true Brennan's style.

A PATIO LUNCH BRENNAN'S STYLE

Ramos Gin Fizz   Beignets
Trout Kottwitz*
Grilled Tomato   Broccoli
Hot French Bread
Bananas Foster   Coffee with Chicory
Wine: Chablis

TROUT KOTTWITZ

  5 tablespoons butter
  8 fillets speckled trout
  1 cup very coarsely chopped artichoke
    bottoms
1¼ cups sliced mushrooms
  ½ teaspoon salt
  ⅛ teaspoon pepper
  ½ cup Brown Sauce
  2 tablespoons lemon juice
  2 cups melted butter (1 pound)

Melt 5 tablespoons butter in a large heavy skillet; add trout, artichokes, and mushrooms and cook 7 to 8 minutes over medium heat, or till fish flakes easily with a fork. Sprinkle with salt and pepper while cooking. Remove fish and vegetables to heated plates, or keep warm in low oven. Combine Brown Sauce, lemon juice, and the 2 cups butter; mix with a wire whisk and cook over low heat until heated through. To serve, ladle about ¼ cup sauce over each fillet. Makes 8 servings.

Brown Sauce: In a saucepan melt 1½ tablespoons *butter;* blend in 1½ tablespoons *all-purpose flour.* Stir in 2 cups *beef broth.* Bring to boiling and cook 3 to 5 minutes. Simmer, uncovered, 30 minutes, stirring occasionally, till sauce is reduced to 1⅓ cups. Use sauce for Trout Kottwitz; store remaining sauce, covered, in refrigerator.

Hint:
Coffee with chicory is the perfect beverage to serve with Bananas Foster. Chicory adds a wonderful aroma and body to coffee. You can buy coffee containing chicory in most large supermarkets or a gourmet food shop. Mix brewed chicory coffee with equal parts of warm milk, and you have café au lait.

Ewald's

Ewald's

Dallas, Texas

As the eldest son of a Düsseldorf restaurant owner, Ewald Scholz was expected to take over the family business in true German fashion. To this end, he began studying the great cuisines of Europe when he was 14 years old. His apprenticeships took him from kitchen to kitchen in Italy, France, and Switzerland, as well as in his native Germany. He eventually crossed the Atlantic to work in several American restaurants, and today he owns the popular Ewald's in Dallas.

A visit to Ewald's would most likely begin with Shrimp du Chef à la Ewald, a Madeira-flavored appetizer with just a hint of garlic. A delightful veal specialty might follow — something of pure French or Italian origin. But in typical Ewaldian style, the recipe may have picked up a Swiss touch here, a German touch there.

When you serve Ewald's Shrimp du Chef at home, make it a special first course or the main dish, but be sure to accompany it with crusty French bread so you can get every last drop of the delicious sauce. The success of this dish depends on cooking the shrimp *only* until they're done. So be sure to select large shrimp for the recipe, about 30 to 35 to the pound. Smaller shrimp are easily overcooked.

A CONTINENTAL DINNER

Shrimp du Chef*
French Bread
Fresh Asparagus   Chive Potatoes
Crème Caramel   Coffee
Wine: Portuguese Rosé

SHRIMP DU CHEF

- 1 tablespoon butter
- 1 tablespoon finely chopped onion
- ½ teaspoon finely chopped garlic
- 20 to 30 large shrimp, cooked, peeled, and deveined
- 2 cups minced fresh mushrooms
  Juice of ½ lemon
- ⅓ cup Madeira wine
- ½ cup Brown Sauce
- 1 tablespoon finely chopped parsley
  Salt
  White pepper
  Lemon wedges
  Parsley sprigs

In a large skillet melt butter; sauté onion and garlic till tender. Add shrimp, mushrooms, and lemon juice; sauté 2 minutes and add wine, Brown Sauce, and parsley. Heat through. Season to taste with salt and white pepper. Remove shrimp from sauce and arrange on plates; cook sauce 1 minute longer and pour over shrimp. Garnish with lemon wedges and parsley. Serve hot with French bread. Makes 4 appetizer or 2 entrée servings.

Brown Sauce: Melt 1½ tablespoons *butter* in a medium saucepan; blend in 1½ tablespoons *all-purpose flour*. Cook and stir over low heat till browned, about 8 to 10 minutes. Stir in 2 cups *beef stock* or *broth*. Bring to boiling and cook 3 to 5 minutes. Reduce heat and simmer, uncovered, 30 minutes, stirring occasionally. Makes about 1½ cups sauce. Store remaining sauce in refrigerator for another use.

Hint:
The trick to cooking fresh asparagus spears is to get the stalks done without overcooking the tips. Lay the spears in a skillet with the tips propped up on a pad of crushed aluminum foil at one side of the pan. Then cook, covered, in a small amount of boiling salted water just till tender, about 10 to 15 minutes.

Bagatelle

Bagatelle

Dallas, Texas

With 30 years of experience in the finest hotels in England, Switzerland, and Panama, Leodegar Meier knows what a restaurant must be to gain a reputation for fine food. Along with Chef Klaus Baumbach, he keeps Bagatelle's patrons returning for more wonderful meals.

The cuisine at Bagatelle is country French. One of their featured dishes is an authentic Canard à la Normande — a very elegant duck recipe prepared in the Normandy way with apple cider and Calvados, or apple brandy. In Normandy, apple cider is the fermented juice of apples. We call it hard cider. But if that is unavailable, fresh or bottled apple juice will provide a similar flavor.

Duck à la Normande is an elegant flamed entrée, perfect for a change-of-pace holiday feast. Yet you'll find this showy attraction is no more effort than the ordinary roasted bird. The ducks are cooked whole, cut in half, and served on a bed of wild rice. This is one dinner your guests will remember long after the holidays end!

A ROAST DUCK HOLIDAY DINNER

Roast Duck à la Normande*   Wild Rice
Broccoli Buds
Warm Yeast Rolls
Compote of Raspberry, Lime, and Lemon
Sherbets
Coffee
Wine: California Merlot

ROAST DUCK À LA NORMANDE

 2 **5- to 6-pound domestic ducks**
 1 **teaspoon salt**
 1 **teaspoon pepper**
 1 **teaspoon dried thyme, crushed**
 4 **large apples**
 1 **quart hot water**
 2 **tablespoons lemon juice**

continued

67

¼ cup cranberry sauce
⅓ cup apple brandy, warmed
Cider Sauce

Sprinkle insides of ducks with salt, pepper, and thyme. Cut *2 apples* into coarse pieces and stuff inside ducks. Place ducks, breast side down, on a rack in a deep roasting pan. Add hot water to pan. Bake ducks in a 400° oven for 1½ hours. Pour off excess liquid and turn ducks breast side up. Continue baking ducks, basting often, till done, about 30 minutes longer. Discard apples inside.

Fill a saucepan or skillet with ½ inch of water; add lemon juice and bring to boiling. Cut remaining 2 apples in half and remove cores. Place in water; cover and simmer just till apples are tender, about 5 minutes. Drain apples and place about 1 tablespoon of cranberry sauce in each half. Prepare Cider Sauce.

To serve, cut ducks in half and arrange on an ovenproof platter with stuffed apples. Heat in 400° oven till hot through, about 10 minutes. Remove from oven and drizzle with warm apple brandy; ignite. Serve with Cider Sauce. Garnish with *parsley,* if desired. Makes 4 servings.

Cider Sauce: Pour excess fat from duck in pan, leaving 3 tablespoons in pan. Add 2 sliced *onions,* and cook till lightly browned. Stir in 3 tablespoons *all-purpose flour* and cook, stirring constantly, 4 to 5 minutes or till browned. Add 2 tablespoons *currant jelly, giblets* from 2 ducks, 1 teaspoon *salt,* ⅛ teaspoon *pepper,* and 2 cups *apple cider.* Bring to boil; reduce heat. Simmer, uncovered, 30 minutes. Strain sauce into a saucepan, discarding giblets. Stir in 1 cup *whipping cream.* Cook and stir till bubbly. Blend in ¼ cup *apple brandy;* heat and serve. Makes 2⅔ cups.

Hint:
The secret of serving dramatic flaming food is to warm the liquor slightly before pouring it over the food. But be careful. Stand back from the platter as you hold the match just above the liquor — the first flames are likely to be high.

London
Chop House

London
Chop House

Detroit, Michigan

Owner Lester Gruber originally called his restaurant the Den of Forty Thieves, and it quickly became a meeting place for artists, musicians, and writers in the early 1930's. It was later expanded and renamed the London Bar, reflecting Lester's growing passion for world travel in search of new ideas in food and wine service. The London Chop House is located in Detroit's busy financial district. It serves as a dining haven in the style of a British gentlemen's club dining room. The restaurant's hearty menu includes items such as fresh California asparagus, imported dover sole roe, cape scallops in puff pastry, and rack of lamb.

One of the more popular entrées served at the London Chop House is their Smoked Beef Omelet, which makes an ideal late-night or Sunday evening supper. The basic recipe makes 2 servings, so you'll need several omelets for a crowd.

A POST-THEATER OMELET SUPPER

Chicken Liver Pâté   Melba Toast
Smoked Beef Omelet*   Brioches
Strawberries Dipped in Chocolate
Espresso   Champagne Cassis

SMOKED BEEF OMELET

2 tablespoons butter
½ of a sweet red pepper, cut into thin strips
½ of a green pepper, cut into thin strips
¼ cup thinly sliced sweet red onion
   Smoked pepper beef, cut into thin strips
   (⅔ cup)
4 eggs, at room temperature
1 tablespoon water
¼ teaspoon salt
2 tablespoons clarified butter
2 tablespoons shredded cheddar cheese
2 tablespoons finely chopped fresh basil
   or parsley

Melt the 2 tablespoons butter in a small skillet.
Add red and green peppers and onion, and
cook just till wilted, about 5 minutes; stir in beef
and remove from heat. Beat eggs, water, and
salt till well blended. Heat clarified butter in a
10-inch skillet or omelet pan over moderately
high heat; pour in egg mixture and cook until
set, lifting edges occasionally to allow un-
cooked portion to run underneath. While
omelet is still moist and soft on top, sprinkle
with cheese and top with vegetable-beef mixture. Fold omelet and place on serving platter.
Garnish with basil or parsley. Makes 2 servings.

Hint:
Strawberries dipped in chocolate make a
delightful dessert or garnish. Wash large, perfect
berries, keeping the hull and stem on the berry.
Melt semisweet chocolate pieces over hot water.
Then dip the berries in the chocolate nearly to
the hull. Chill until serving time on a waxed
paper-lined tray or cookie sheet.

Ah Wok

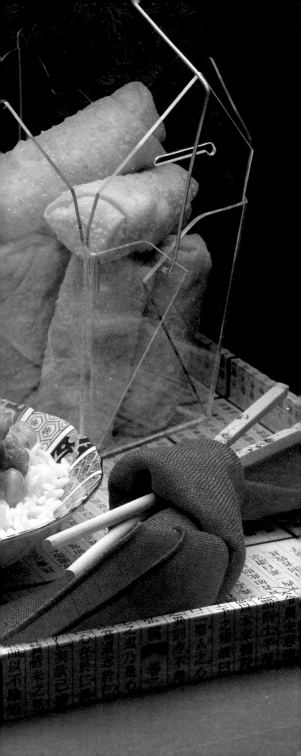

Ah Wok

Novi, Michigan

For 35 years, Moi N. Gam earned an outstanding reputation as a chef in several top New York Chinese restaurants. Then, his sons coaxed him into establishing a family restaurant in Novi, Michigan, just outside Detroit. Once the move was made, their Ah Wok Restaurant met with immediate success.

Today, customers travel for miles to visit this unique eating spot, choosing from a variety of Mandarin-Cantonese dishes made with seafood, duck, chicken, or pork. One of the most tempting dishes is their zesty Peanut Chicken.

Unlike most stir-fry recipes, Peanut Chicken requires very little slicing and chopping. You can buy boned chicken breasts to reduce preparation time even more. The seasoning leans toward the spicy Szechwan style, so gather together your most adventurous friends to share in this culinary experience. Since the preparation is minimal, you can have a dinner party at a moment's notice. A quick stop for chicken, egg rolls, fortune cookies, and mai tai mix, and you've got the party in hand!

A SIMPLE STIR-FRY DINNER

Mai Tai Cocktails
Chinese Egg Rolls
Sweet Sour Sauce   Hot Mustard Sauce
Peanut Chicken*   Rice
Fortune Cookies   Tea
Beer or Wan Fu wine

PEANUT CHICKEN

    5 chicken breasts, boned
    6 egg whites (1 cup)
    6 tablespoons cornstarch
2¼ cups cooking oil

continued

½ cup fresh roasted peanuts
¼ cup sliced water chestnuts
¼ cup green peas
¼ cup diced bamboo shoots
¾ cup chicken broth
1 teaspoon bottled hot pepper sauce
½ teaspoon sugar
½ teaspoon salt
½ teaspoon monosodium glutamate
½ teaspoon sesame oil
¼ teaspoon dried hot pepper, crushed
½ cup cold water

Cut chicken into 1-inch slices. Combine egg whites, *4 tablespoons* of the cornstarch, and *1 tablespoon* of the oil; mix well. Pour over chicken and marinate for 1 hour. In wok or large saucepan heat *2 cups* of the oil till very hot (365°). With slotted spoon lift about ¼ of the chicken from the marinade and fry in hot oil for 2 minutes; drain and set aside. Repeat with remaining chicken. In another wok heat remaining 3 tablespoons oil over high heat. Add peanuts and vegetables; stir-fry 2 minutes. Add chicken and broth. Bring mixture to a full boil. Add hot pepper sauce, sugar, monosodium glutamate, sesame oil, hot pepper, and salt. Blend the remaining 2 tablespoons cornstarch with cold water and add to boiling mixture. Cook, stirring constantly, till thickened and bubbly. Serve over *rice*. Makes 4 generous servings.

Hint:
When using chopsticks, one chopstick remains fixed, the other moves, and together they act like tongs. Hold the first stick between the base of your thumb and the tip of your ring finger. Place the second stick between your thumb tip and the tips of your index and middle fingers. Keep the ends even and move the second stick against the first to pick up food.

The Berghoff

The Berghoff

Chicago, Illinois

America's "second city" is an exciting town filled with many first-rate dining spots. One such colorful place is The Berghoff Restaurant, where the third generation of the Berghoff family is serving the same homemade foods that pleased the first customers back in 1898. This famous Chicago Loop restaurant has full-meal lunches that are area crowd-pleasers, and its high-ceilinged oaken dining rooms are always bustling with activity.

The menu at The Berghoff offers an assortment of authentic German-Austrian dishes including the traditional wiener schnitzel, liver dumpling soup, Bismarck herring, and sauerbraten with potato pancakes, as well as some less familiar foods.

Their Ragout à la Deutsch — beef tenderloin tips Bavarian style — is a hearty meat and vegetable entrée.

A CASUAL GERMAN-STYLE SUPPER

Ragout à la Deutsch*
Steamed Cabbage   Cooked Carrots
Rye Bread   Butter
Warm Apple Strudel
Iced Tea   Beer

RAGOUT À LA DEUTSCH

1¾ pounds sirloin, cut into ¼-inch strips
3 tablespoons butter, melted
3 tablespoons all-purpose flour
½ cup white wine
¾ cup green peppers, diced
1 medium onion, diced
1½ cups sliced mushrooms
1 4-ounce jar sliced pimiento, drained
1 teaspoon salt
Dash bottled hot pepper sauce
Dash Worcestershire sauce

In a skillet cook sirloin in *2 tablespoons* of the melted butter just until browned, about 5 minutes. Pour drippings into a measuring cup; skim 2 tablespoons drippings off top and place in a saucepan. Add flour and blend well. Cook and stir over low heat till bubbly, about 1 minute; remove from heat. Add water to meat juices remaining in measuring cup to make 1 cup; add to flour mixture and blend well. Cook over medium heat, stirring constantly, till thickened, about 5 minutes. Stir in wine and set aside.

In same skillet cook green pepper, onion, and mushrooms in remaining 1 tablespoon butter just till tender, about 5 minutes. Add beef, gravy, pimiento, salt, hot pepper sauce, and Worcestershire sauce. Bring to boiling and simmer 30 minutes. Makes 5 servings.

Hint:
If you plan to serve beer with the meal, or if you would like a more robust ragout, take a cooking tip from the Germans and substitute your favorite beer for the white wine in the recipe. Use the same amount of beer and add according to the directions for wine.

Gordon

Gordon

Chicago, Illinois

Gordon Sinclair turned a small cafe in an aging Chicago hotel into a smart, sophisticated restaurant of nouvelle cuisine. Here you're likely to find such imaginative items as artichoke fritters with Béarnaise sauce, duckling en croûte with prunes and pistachios, sole mousse with shrimp and crab meat, all manner of crispy, crunchy vegetables and salads, and irresistibly gorgeous desserts.

One of Gordon's typically enticing desserts is Kiwi and Strawberry Tart, a creamy orange-flavored custard in a pastry shell topped with an arrangement of bright red strawberries and pastel green kiwi slices. This refreshing dessert is so special, you'll want to make it the featured attraction at your next get-together.

All you do is prepare the pastry shell, fill it with the custard mixture, and bake. Once cooled, arrange a row of fresh strawberries around the outside edge and fill the center with a layer of kiwi slices. Then brush the top with warm apricot jam. It's simple to make, and sure to be a sensation whenever it is served.

GARDEN DINNER ON THE PORCH

Broiled Chicken Breasts
Sautéed Snow Peas   Sliced Tomatoes
Warm Muffins
Kiwi and Strawberry Tart*   Iced Coffee
Wine: Chenin Blanc

KIWI AND STRAWBERRY TART

    Pastry for one 9-inch pie
1½ cups whipping cream
 ½ cup sugar
 3 egg yolks
 1 teaspoon vanilla *or* 2 tablespoons
    Cointreau
1½ to 2 cups whole fresh strawberries
 1 kiwi, sliced
 ¼ cup apricot jam

Roll out pastry to ⅛-inch thickness; fit into a
9-inch false-bottom flan pan. Line bottom with
aluminum foil and fill center with dried beans,
rice, or pie weights. Bake in a 425° oven till
sides brown and puff away from pan, about 12
minutes. Remove weights and foil; cool pastry
shell.

In a bowl combine cream, sugar, egg yolks,
and vanilla or Cointreau. Pour into cooled pastry shell and bake in 325° oven till firm, about
35 minutes. Cool completely. Arrange a row of
strawberries around outside edge of tart. Fill
inside area with a single layer of kiwi. Heat jam
just till melted and brush over fruit with a pastry
brush. Makes 10 to 12 servings.

Hint:
Kiwi is a delicately flavored fruit imported from
New Zealand. It looks rather odd with its fuzzy
brown skin, green flesh, and numerous small
black seeds inside. But it has a pleasingly
unique flavor. To enjoy its tart-sweet interior,
just peel the fuzzy skin and slice or cube.

Mader's

Mader's

Milwaukee, Wisconsin

Mader's Castle Restaurant really is a castle — or at least it looks like one! This popular eating spot is filled with relics of feudal Germany such as swords, armor, and shields, as well as a collection of beer steins. In keeping with tradition, Mader's still serves food in the same grand German style as it did when it first opened its doors in 1902.

Because so many loyal Mader's customers have asked for family recipes through the years, the owners finally published their own cookbook. One of the very favorites in their collection is Black Forest Cherry Torte, a wonderfully light, brandy-flavored cake.

The dessert's full German name is *Schwartzwalder Kirschtorte*, and the best brandy to use for the flavoring is kirsch, that white brandy of Alsace, Switzerland, and Germany's Black Forest region. Elegant as it is, this delectable dessert is as easy to make as an ordinary chocolate cake, and it makes an impressive finalé to any menu.

A BIRTHDAY SUPPER

Fresh Asparagus with Lemon Mayonnaise
Cold Smoked Turkey and Ham
Hot German Potato Salad
Sliced Tomatoes
Black Forest Cherry Torte*   Cappuccino
Wine: Mosel Riesling

BLACK FOREST CHERRY TORTE

- ¾ cup all-purpose flour
- ¼ cup cocoa
- ¼ teaspoon salt
- 6 eggs, separated
- 1 teaspoon vanilla
- 1¼ cups sugar

continued

87

½ **teaspoon cream of tartar**
Brandy Glaze
Whipped Cream Frosting
Shaved milk chocolate
Maraschino cherries, well drained

Combine flour, cocoa, and salt; sift together several times and set aside. In small mixer bowl beat egg yolks and vanilla till thick and lemon colored. Gradually add ¾ cup of the sugar; continue beating till thick and light, about 6 minutes total. Set aside. Thoroughly wash beaters. In large mixer bowl beat egg whites and cream of tartar till soft peaks form. Gradually add the remaining ½ cup sugar, beating till sugar dissolves and stiff peaks form. Fold egg yolk mixture into egg white mixture. Sift flour mixture over egg mixture and fold in gently but thoroughly. Turn batter into 2 ungreased deep 9-inch round cake pans. Bake in 350° oven about 25 minutes or till cake tests done. Invert pans on racks to cool. When completely cool, loosen sides and remove from pans. Meanwhile, prepare Brandy Glaze; brush over top of cake layers. Prepare Whipped Cream Frosting and spread on tops of both cake layers; stack, top sides up, and frost sides. Sprinkle with shaved chocolate and garnish with cherries. Chill well before serving. Store in refrigerator. Makes 12 servings.

   Brandy Glaze: In a small saucepan combine ⅓ cup *sugar* and 4 teaspoons *water.* Cook and stir over low heat till sugar dissolves. Remove from heat and cool slightly; add ⅓ cup *brandy.*

   Whipped Cream Frosting: Combine 2 cups *whipping cream* and ¼ cup *powdered sugar;* chill well. Beat till thick and light; add 2 tablespoons *brandy.*

Hint:
For a continental touch, serve steaming cups of cappuccino. To make this delicious drink, pour equal parts of espresso and very hot milk into cups. Then add a cinnamon stick and dash of nutmeg topping.

The
New French
Café

The New French Café

Minneapolis, Minnesota

Lynne Alpert and Pamela Sherman, two native Minnesotans, first met and became friends when they were living in France. This friendship led them to transform an old Minneapolis warehouse into The New French Café — a charming eating spot with the elegant simplicity of natural brick walls, butcher block tables, and bentwood chairs.

In an effort to duplicate the restaurants of France, all fruits, vegetables, meats, and fish served are fresh, and everything on the menu is prepared from scratch on the premises. Over 130 loaves of bread and 300 croissants are baked fresh daily! One special attraction of the cafe is the exposed kitchen where foods are given their finishing touches and special orders are prepared in full view of the customers.

The food served at The New French Café is in the nouvelle cuisine style and, like the decor, it is both elegant and simple. One delicious appetizer is Seviche à la Française, a raw fish dish that was invented in Peru and is served in most Latin American countries. The dish is prepared by marinating raw fish in lime juice with onions, radishes, and mushrooms. This marinade "cooks" the fish, changing the texture and flavor. It makes an out-of-the-ordinary appetizer or a refreshing luncheon entrée.

A SPRINGTIME LUNCHEON

Cream of Asparagus Soup
Seviche à la Française*
Croissants
Brie Cheese with Fresh Fruit
Wine: White Burgundy or Chardonnay

SEVICHE À LA FRANÇAISE

- 1 pound fresh scallops, salmon, *or* grey sole
- 1 cup freshly squeezed lime juice
- 4 large, firm mushroom caps
- 2 radishes
- 1 green onion
- 3 to 4 tablespoons olive oil
- 1 tablespoon white wine vinegar
  Cayenne pepper
- 12 large flat spinach leaves *or* Boston *or* Bibb lettuce leaves
- 1 tablespoon lumpfish caviar

Use only very fresh scallops or fish. Wash scallops thoroughly to remove any sand, and slice into ¼-inch-thick disks (cut fish into same size pieces). Place in a shallow layer in a large glass dish. *Cover* with lime juice and marinate 30 minutes at room temperature or until scallops or fish turn opaque. Drain off lime juice and discard.

Trim mushrooms into squares and slice off gills; cut mushrooms into matchstick-size strips. Slice radishes and cut into matchstick-size strips. Slice green portion only of onion into ¼-inch rounds. Combine olive oil and vinegar with a whisk and pour over scallops or fish. Taste and add more oil if needed. Sprinkle with cayenne. Just before serving, toss scallops with mushrooms, radishes, and onion. Mound on spinach- or lettuce-lined plates and sprinkle with caviar. Garnish plates with *radishes* and *carrots,* if desired. Makes 4 servings.

Hint:
The seviche should be served very cold. To assure this, place your serving dishes in the freezer to chill before the guests arrive. Then arrange the seviche atop spinach leaves and add a sprinkling of caviar for a touch of French elegance.

Star
of the Sea Room

Star of the Sea Room
San Diego, California

No wonder the fish and seafood taste so fresh at the Star of the Sea Room — they practically flip from the ocean right onto the grill! In fact, the restaurant's owners, the Ghio family, operate their own fishing fleet, both wholesale and retail fish markets, and a number of other dining spots. Among the best of these is the regal Star of the Sea Room, a fish-loving gourmet's paradise with a sparkling view of San Diego Bay.

The decor of this legendary seafood spot is elegant — cream-colored table linens, rich wood hues mixed with gleaming gold, and a huge crystal chandelier. Even the menu is dazzling, with many delicacies fresh from the sea.

In this San Diego restaurant or in your own home, Star of the Sea Salad can be an intriguing first course, or it can act as the focus of an entire meal. The secret of this simple salad is its sweet creamy dressing, a unique blend of curry and golden raisins. Make the topping at your convenience and refrigerate it to let the flavors mellow. But freshness is a must for the shellfish, so plan to shop at the local fish market and enjoy this delightful salad all in the same day.

A SEAFARING SUPPER

Star of the Sea Salad*
Hard Rolls
Honeydew Melon with Raspberries
Coffee
Wine: Pouilly Fuisse

95

STAR OF THE SEA SALAD

- ½ cup mayonnaise
- ¼ cup milk
- 2 tablespoons white or golden raisins
- 1 tablespoon sugar
- 1 teaspoon mild curry powder
- 1 teaspoon lemon juice
- 1 teaspoon red wine vinegar
- 1 teaspoon cocktail sauce
- 4 hearts of romaine, torn (about 8 cups)
- 1 pound cooked shrimp, lobster, *or* king crab legs, *or* a combination

Combine mayonnaise, milk, raisins, sugar, curry powder, lemon juice, vinegar, and cocktail sauce; blend well. Chill. Peel or shell seafood; cut lobster and crab into bite-size pieces. When ready to serve, toss dressing with romaine and seafood. Makes 4 main dish or 8 appetizer servings.

Hint:
Giant scallop shells are ideal serving bowls for the salad and dressing, but there are many suitable substitutes. A soup tureen or large footed compote can double as a salad bowl. Or, fill an ice bucket half full of crushed ice and line it with lettuce, then top with the salad.

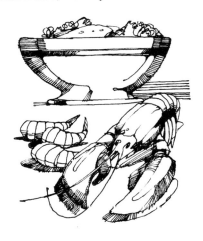

Le Dôm

Le Dôme

Los Angeles, California

Le Dôme made its debut in 1978 as a contemporary version of a southern French brasserie. The owners had originally envisioned a true brasserie, a small, convivial restaurant serving simple, provincial food. But since Le Dôme opened its doors, it has grown both in concept and reality. This chic cafe on Sunset Boulevard features a "domed" round bar with five dining rooms radiating from its center. The interior is an updated version of Art Nouveau — dark green walls and carpet, rich oil paintings, and plush seating throughout. It is a truly original restaurant that serves an exciting, bold cuisine. Each course is a lesson in fine dining, and the desserts are just as exciting as the appetizers.

One such special dessert is Clafoutis aux Cerises (kla-FOO-tee o ser-EZ). In the provinces, clafoutis is known as a rather "homely" dessert made by pouring a pancake-like batter over sweet cherries. Then the mixture is baked and served with fresh cream. At Le Dôme, however, Clafoutis aux Cerises is a glamorous treat. The batter becomes a creamy custard baked in a buttery egg pastry. A true gourmet item!

Though the dessert can be baked in a standard pie pan, a shallow flan or tart pan transforms it into a showy continental classic. It makes an impressive addition to any buffet spread and an easy-to-serve dessert.

A COLD SUMMER BUFFET

Cold Poached Salmon with Mayonnaise
Spinach Salad
Chilled New Potatoes with Dill
Croissants
Clafoutis aux Cerises*   Coffee
Wine: California Pinot Noir Blanc

CLAFOUTIS AUX CERISES

   Pâte Brisée
4 **eggs, beaten**
1 **cup sugar**
½ **cup whipping cream**
1 **cup milk, scalded**
1 **pound fresh sweet cherries, pitted**

Line an 11-inch metal flan pan with Pâte Brisée; flute edges high. Line with aluminum foil and fill center with pie weights or dried beans. Bake in 400° oven for 10 minutes. Remove foil and beans. Combine eggs, sugar, and whipping cream; gradually add hot milk, beating constantly with a wire whisk till blended. Place cherries in baked pastry shell and pour custard over cherries. Bake in 350° oven for 35 minutes or till knife inserted 1 inch from outside edge comes out clean. Cool completely. (Center will set as custard cools.) If desired, serve with *cream* or *whipped cream*. Makes 6 servings.

Pâte Brisée: Combine 1½ cups *all-purpose flour*, ¼ teaspoon *salt*, and ¼ teaspoon *sugar*. With a pastry blender, cut in 6 tablespoons *butter* cut into ½-inch cubes, and 3 tablespoons chilled *shortening*, till pieces are the size of small peas. Sprinkle in ¼ cup *ice water*, 1 tablespoon at a time, and toss with a fork till all flour is moistened. Press dough into a ball and dust lightly with flour; wrap in waxed paper and chill at least 2 hours. Place dough on a lightly floured board and let stand 5 minutes. If dough is hard, hit with a rolling pin to flatten. Roll out dough to a ⅛-inch thickness and fit into pan.

Hint:
If you don't have a fish poacher, cook the salmon in a roaster with a lid. Place the fish in the pan with several onion and lemon slices and celery stalks. Add stock or salted water, cover and bring to a boil. Reduce the heat and simmer for 5 to 8 minutes per pound. Remove the fish from the liquid. Leave the head and tail intact; working with the grain, skin and trim the fish.

Ma Maison

Ma Maison

Los Angeles, California

Though it looks more like a charming sandwich shop than one of Los Angeles' hottest dining spots, Ma Maison boasts some of Hollywood's most famous actors, directors, producers, and writers among its loyal patrons. The surroundings are eclectic; the food is exquisite and remains the main attraction. Genuine French country cooking predominates, with country-style pâtés, crudités, rich onion soup, salad Niçoise, steamed fish, and quiche as standard fare. At meal's end the desserts are as tempting to eat as they are lovely to look at.

One star attraction of the dessert menu that you will enjoy preparing for friends is Ma Maison's Lemon-Raspberry Tart. Fresh raspberries never had it so good — or so elegant. The sugar cookie-like crust is baked first, then filled with rich, lemony custard and fresh raspberries. Warmed raspberry jam makes a shimmering glaze.

A COUNTRY FRENCH PICNIC

Raw Vegetables with Yogurt-Lemon Dip
Pâté   French Bread
Cold Grilled Chicken
Lemon-Raspberry Tart*
Wine: Beaujolais or California Gamay

LEMON-RASPBERRY TART

   Pâte Sucrée
 4 eggs, slightly beaten
 ¾ cup sugar
 ¼ cup butter
 ¼ cup whipping cream

continued

½   cup lemon juice
3   tablespoons orange juice
2   pints raspberries
½   cup raspberry jelly

Make Pâte Sucrée and chill overnight. In a heavy saucepan combine eggs, sugar, butter, cream, lemon juice, and orange juice. Cook over medium heat, stirring constantly, until mixture is thick and smooth, about 8 minutes. Remove from heat; cover with clear plastic wrap.

On well-floured surface, roll out Pâte Sucrée to fit a 10-inch pie plate or flan pan; fit into pan and trim pastry even with edge of pie plate. Work rapidly so dough does not become warm and difficult to handle. Line with aluminum foil and fill center with dried beans, rice, or pie weights. Bake in a 350° oven for 15 minutes. Remove foil and beans; bake 5 minutes longer. Fill baked pastry with lemon filling. Cover edges of pastry with foil to prevent overbrowning. Return to oven and bake 15 minutes or till filling is set. Cool on rack. Arrange berries on top of pie. Heat jelly in a small saucepan and brush generously over raspberries. Makes 8 servings.

Pâte Sucrée: In mixing bowl combine 2½ cups *flour*, 1¼ cups *sugar*, and a pinch *salt*; cut in 1¼ cups *butter* till mixture resembles crumbs. Add 3 slightly beaten *eggs*, mixing to form a very soft dough. Cover and chill overnight. Divide dough in half. Wrap one half in moisture-vaporproof wrapping and freeze for later use. Roll other half as desired.

Hint:
For a perfect pastry shell with no broken sides, use a flan pan with removable collar. After the pastry is baked, the collar can be loosened and removed, assuring a perfect crust. These removable collar flan pans are available in most cookware departments and gourmet shops.

Yamato

Yamato

San Francisco, California

Japanese cooks "frame" food as they would
a painting — so it appeals to the eye, and in
turn, to the palate. You expect to find attractive
food served in this manner at Yamato Sukiyaki
House, and you are never disappointed. A
bonus is the attractive dining arrangement with
rooms of varying sizes opening into one another
on many levels.

Japanese sukiyaki is a house specialty, but
the tempura featured at Yamato is equally
delicious. To make the tempura, dip fish, seafood, and an assortment of fresh vegetables in a
light batter. Then deep fry to perfection until the
batter forms a lacelike crust. These crispy mor-
sels are served with a flavorful tempura sauce.

Tempura can be an exciting party focus for a
small gathering of 4 to 6. An electric wok, a
deep electric skillet, or fondue pot may be used
for cooking. By having each guest cook his own
food right at the table, this delicious tempura
gets the attention it deserves.

A JAPANESE DINNER

Wonton Soup
Tempura*   Rice
Mandarin Orange Sections with Juice
Green Tea
Wine: Saki

TEMPURA

- ¾ **pound fish fillets, cut into 1½x2-inch
  pieces**
- 12 **shrimp *or* prawns, cleaned and
  butterflied (with tails on)**
- 6 **scallops**
- 1 **sweet potato *or* 3 carrots, peeled and cut
  into ¼-inch diagonal slices**
- 1 **small eggplant *or* 2 zucchini, unpeeled
  and cut into ¼-inch slices**

continued

107

¼ **pound green beans** *or* **asparagus tips,**
   cut into bite-size pieces
   Cooking oil for deep-fat frying
3 **cups cake flour**
1 **tablespoon baking powder**
2 **egg yolks**
2 **cups ice water**
   Tempura Sauce

Drain seafood and vegetables thoroughly on paper towels. Arrange food on large platter. Cover and chill. Pour several inches of vegetable oil into an *electric* wok, deep skillet, or fondue pot set on serving table; heat to 400°. Meanwhile sift flour and baking powder together. Thoroughly beat egg yolks with a wire whisk or rotary beater; blend in water. Sprinkle flour evenly over liquid and beat with whisk just until flour is moistened and large lumps disappear. (Batter should have small lumps and be the consistency of whipping cream.) *Do not stir batter after it is mixed.*

Dip seafood and vegetables in batter and drain slightly; place in individual frying baskets and fry in hot oil till lightly browned, about 3 or 4 minutes. (Fry only a few items at a time or oil will boil over.) Repeat with remaining ingredients, skimming bits of cooked batter off oil as necessary. If desired, batter and fry some sprigs of *parsley* for garnish. Drain tempura on paper towels. Serve with Tempura Sauce for dipping and, if desired, grated fresh *radish*. Makes 6 servings.

Tempura Sauce: In a small saucepan combine ½ cup *dashi* (Japanese fish stock), ¼ cup *soy sauce*, 2 teaspoons *sugar*, and a dash of *monosodium glutamate*. Heat through. Makes ¾ cup.

Hint:
For a festive tempura platter, choose only fresh vegetables, keeping in mind their color and texture. To preserve fresh vegetable color and to prevent darkening, sprinkle with lemon juice. Be sure all the vegetables are dry before dipping in the batter so the coating will cling evenly.

Perry's

Perry's

San Francisco, California

When you visit Perry's and sit down at a table, your waiter directs your glance to the boldly painted menu on the wall. It's all part of the casual attitude and colorful decor of this popular San Francisco restaurant. There's a wide assortment of unbeatable favorites — lasagne, quiche, omelets, corned beef hash, skewered lamb, and much more. Even the hamburgers are sophisticated treats. And who could pass up a cup of cappuccino — one of San Francisco's favorite coffee drinks.

Perry's presents a delightful Saturday and Sunday brunch, and their Eggs Blackstone, a unique variation of Eggs Benedict, is an excellent choice for midday dining. It also fits the bill as a satisfying, yet basic, choice after a "later-than-we-thought" night on the town.

A SUNDAY NIGHT SUPPER

Papaya with Raspberries
Eggs Blackstone*
Carrot Cake   Coffee Royale
Wine: Muscat Canelli

EGGS BLACKSTONE

- 4 **English muffins**
- 8 **eggs**
- 8 **½-inch slices tomato**
- 1 **tablespoon butter**
- 16 **slices bacon, crisp-cooked and crumbled**
  Hollandaise Sauce

Split muffins with a fork; toast. Poach eggs to desired doneness in simmering water. While eggs cook, melt butter in a skillet over medium heat; brown tomato slices on both sides in butter. Place a tomato slice on each muffin half and sprinkle with some of the crumbled bacon. Place a poached egg on top and cover generously with Hollandaise Sauce. Sprinkle lightly with remaining bacon and serve immediately. Makes 4 servings.

Hollandaise Sauce: Cut 1 cup of *butter* into 12 equal pieces. In top of double boiler combine 4 *egg yolks,* 3 tablespoons *lemon juice,* and 4 *pieces* of the butter; place over simmering water and stir rapidly with a wire whisk till butter melts. Add remaining butter 1 piece at a time, stirring till each melts before adding another. Add a dash of *cayenne* and serve immediately. (If sauce starts to thicken before it is served, add a small amount of boiling water while stirring.) Makes 1½ cups.

Hint:
Serve a dessert coffee instead of dessert or in place of an after-dinner liqueur. For Coffee Royale, add 2 tablespoons of brandy to ½ cup hot strong coffee. Garnish with a dollop of whipped cream and sprinkle with grated orange peel.

Ernie's

Ernie's

San Francisco, California

Ernie's is an elegant San Francisco restaurant that frequently "stars" in movie and television scenes that call for a sophisticated dining spot. The restaurant is truly a Victorian gem with three impeccable dining rooms colored in a rich burgundy with silk brocade on the walls, velvet chairs, and plush carpeting. Gleaming crystal, polished brass, and mirrored surfaces dazzle the eye.

But Ernie's is much more than a lovely, historic showplace. The restaurant is celebrated for fine food and outstanding service. Their young chef, Jacky Robert, enjoys adding exciting new dishes to Ernie's predominantly French cuisine.

Chicken Cynthia à la Champagne is typical of Robert's flair for creating superb flavor harmonies in basically simple dishes. By adding champagne and orange liqueur to the classic ingredients of chicken, mushrooms, and cream, he has developed a truly epicurean dish.

The chicken is first baked, then gently simmered in champagne and curaçao. Mushrooms and cream are added to make a rich sauce, then the chicken and sauce are arranged in a chafing dish for an impressive main course.

A CHAMPAGNE DINNER

Pâté   Melba Toast
Chicken Cynthia à la Champagne*
Parsley Rice   Orange and Grape Compote
Cheese Platter   Crusty French Bread
Wine: Brut Champagne

CHICKEN CYNTHIA À LA CHAMPAGNE

- 3 tablespoons all-purpose flour
- 1 teaspoon salt
- 2 chicken breasts, skinned, boned, and halved
- 4 chicken thighs, skinned and boned
- 1 tablespoon butter
- 1 tablespoon cooking oil
- 2 tablespoons curaçao
- ¾ cup dry champagne
- 1 cup chicken bouillon
- 1 cup sliced fresh mushrooms
- 1 tablespoon butter, melted
- ½ cup whipping cream
  Orange wedges
  Seedless grapes

Combine flour and salt; coat chicken pieces in flour mixture. Heat 1 tablespoon butter and oil in a large skillet. Add chicken and cook for 5 minutes on each side. Place chicken in 9x9x2-inch baking pan and bake in a 350° oven, uncovered, for 20 minutes. Pour fat from skillet and add curaçao, champagne, and bouillon; bring just to a simmer. Add chicken and simmer, uncovered, for 20 minutes or till tender. Cook mushrooms in 1 tablespoon butter; add to chicken along with cream. Spoon into a chafing dish and garnish with orange wedges and grapes, or serve fruits in compotes. Makes 4 servings.

Hint:
Don't hesitate to ask the wine shop for advice on selecting champagne. Handle the bottles carefully and allow them to rest on their sides for a few days before serving. This keeps the cork wet and ensures an airtight seal which preserves the quality of the wine. Serve champagne very cold, and open it gently with a towel over the cork. Avoid shaking the bottle.

Washington Square Bar & Grill

Washington Square Bar & Grill

San Francisco, California

This popular cafe employs veteran Italian chefs who excel in San Francisco's gustatorial specialties — fresh fish, veal, and pastas. The decor here is classic American bar and grill with iron-oxide walls, tuxedoed waiters and white napery. Music at the Washington Square Bar & Grill is muted and very choice with the legendary saloon pianists Burt Bales, Norma Teagarden, and John Horton Cooper performing. Always on hand are owners Sam Deitsch and Ed Moose, greeting guests who frequently include writers, painters, actors, and politicians.

The Vegetarian Joe is the Washington Square Bar & Grill's version of a San Francisco classic, Joe's Special. As the story goes, the first Special was put together at the demand of a hungry celebrity when Joe, proprietor of a popular eatery, had run short of food. The original recipe included ground beef, vegetables, eggs, and cheese. The meatless version was added to the Washington Square Bar & Grill menu to please a growing number of vegetarian customers. You'll find it an exquisitely healthy dish brimming with crispy, crunchy vegetables of all kinds.

Select whatever vegetables are in season — asparagus, broccoli, carrots, celery, cauliflower, peppers, snow peas, squash. Be sure to use only fresh produce, as frozen or canned vegetables "water out" during cooking.

A SPEEDY VEGETARIAN SUPPER

Cold Cucumber-Yogurt Soup
The Vegetarian Joe*
Cracked Wheat Muffins
Peach Melba   Tea
Wine: Italian Soave or California Riesling

THE VEGETARIAN JOE

1½ to 2 cups mixed *fresh* vegetables
1 cup chopped red, white, and green onion
2 to 3 tablespoons olive oil *or* melted butter
2 cloves garlic, pressed
4 ounces fresh leaf spinach
1 cup sliced fresh mushrooms *and/or* steamed eggplant cubes
6 eggs
¼ teaspoon minced fresh herb (parsley, basil, oregano, chives, mint, coriander, cilantro, or sprouted onion tops)
Dash of chicken bouillon granules or ½ teaspoon salt *or* seasoned salt
Dash freshly ground pepper to taste
½ cup grated cheddar cheese (optional)
2 tablespoons butter

Slice, chop, shred, or section mixed vegetables as desired. Steam vegetables just till crisp-tender (shredded vegetables and sprouts may be used raw). Sauté onion in olive oil or butter; stir in garlic. Place spinach in separate saucepan; cover and cook over medium-high heat just till spinach wilts, about 1 to 2 minutes. Squeeze spinach dry and chop. Combine onion mixture, spinach, mushrooms or eggplant, and mixed vegetables. In mixing bowl beat eggs together with herbs, salt, and pepper. Toss with vegetable mixture. Add cheese, if desired. Melt butter in a large skillet. Add egg mixture and cook over medium-high heat, stirring gently, until eggs are set, about 4 minutes. Makes 4 servings.

Hint:
Look over the teas available at your market and try some new blends and combinations. Or, brew some herb teas. Make tea in small quantities with fresh boiling water and serve it very hot for the best flavor and aroma. Garnish with a twist of lemon.

The
Golden Lion

The Golden Lion

Seattle, Washington

The dining room at The Golden Lion is frequently set aglow with lively flames as Chef Martin Uddenberg ignites his marvelous food creations tableside. The culinary fireworks are an integral part of such favorite dishes as Steak Diane, Veal Calvados, and Breast of Chicken Shangri-La. Desserts are set aflame as well — specialties such as Baked Alaska and Crepes Jasper.

Another of Chef Uddenberg's specialties is Celery Victor, an artfully arranged salad of tomatoes, egg slices, and tender crab meat, accented with marinated celery and a garnish of avocado, lemon, and black olives.

When summer's heat dulls appetites, the pleasing combination of contrasting colors, flavors, and textures of Celery Victor will tempt the palate as well as the eye.

A SUMMER SALAD SUPPER

Celery Victor*
Crusty Rolls   Butter
Bing Cherries   Honey-Yogurt Dip
Wine: Liebfraumilch

CELERY VICTOR

- 1 **bunch celery**
- 1 **slice bacon**
- ½ **carrot, sliced**
- ½ **teaspoon salt**
- 3 **cups chicken broth**
  Gourmet Dressing
- 1 **head Bibb or butter lettuce**
- 18 **cooked king crab legs**
- 6 **tomatoes, sliced**
- 6 **hard-cooked eggs, sliced**
- 2 **avocados, peeled and cut into thirds**

continued

Lemon wedges
Black olives
Parsley sprigs

Leaving celery bunch in one piece, trim off upper leaves and wash thoroughly; drain. Place celery in a large oven-proof skillet or Dutch oven; add bacon, carrot, salt, and broth. Bring to a boil. Cover and place in a 350° oven for 20 minutes, or till celery is tender. Remove from oven and cool. Chill celery overnight in broth. Drain; discard broth. Cut celery bunch into 3-inch pieces; slice pieces lengthwise into thin strips. Marinate in Gourmet Dressing for 3 hours. Drain, reserving dressing.

Line 6 plates with lettuce leaves and place marinated celery in center of each plate; arrange crab legs, tomato slices, egg slices, and avocado around celery. Garnish with lemon, olives, and parsley. Serve with reserved Gourmet Dressing. Makes 6 servings.

Gourmet Dressing: In a blender container combine ½ cup *vinegar, tarragon vinegar,* or *red wine,* 1½ teaspoons *celery salt,* 1½ teaspoons *chicken bouillon granules,* 1 teaspoon *salt,* ½ teaspoon *crushed black pepper,* ¼ teaspoon *dry mustard,* and 1 tablespoon *lemon juice.* Blend until mixed. Gradually add 1½ cups *salad oil,* blending well. Stir or shake well before using. Makes 1 pint.

Hint:
This simple summer menu easily adapts to almost any outdoor setting. Pack the unassembled ingredients in separate plastic pouches. To serve, remove the celery from the marinade, arrange the salad on a plate, and use the remaining marinade as dressing.

Nendel's

Nendel's
Portland, Oregon

There is a lot of native pride in the foods served at Nendel's in Portland, and the menu reflects the variety of great-tasting foods indigenous to the Pacific Northwest. Columbia River salmon and sturgeon, Olympia oysters and clams, and the succulent crabs of the cold north waters are regular menu features in season. Oregon's remarkable fresh fruits and Washington's wines also find a spot on Nendel's menu.

When the restaurant first opened in the 1930's a typical dinner consisted of hearty pan-fried foods. Today, Nendel's still serves these foods, but has added such varied menu entries as Mandarin pork and cheesecake.

One of their outstanding dishes is Chicken Livers Sautéed. At home, it's an ideal hot hors d'oeuvre for casual entertaining where light snacks and tasty beverages are enjoyed. This delightful blend of chicken livers, mushrooms, onions, and a hint of sherry is a snap to prepare. So invite the office crowd over after work for wine spritzers or kir. Bring out the Chicken Livers Sautéed and some simple snacks, and you have everything you need to keep good conversation flowing.

AN IMPROMPTU HORS D'OEUVRES BAR

Chicken Livers Sautéed*   Toast Rounds
Spinach Cheese Balls
Broccoli Buds and Carrot Curls
Assorted Crackers
Kir or Wine Spritzers

CHICKEN LIVERS SAUTÉED

1 medium onion, sliced
1 cup sliced fresh mushrooms
½ cup butter
½ cup dry sherry
  Salt
  Pepper
  Monosodium glutamate
2 tablespoons cooking oil
½ cup all-purpose flour
½ teaspoon salt
1 pound chicken livers

In medium skillet sauté onion and mushrooms in butter just until tender, about 4 minutes. Add sherry; sprinkle with salt, pepper, and monosodium glutamate. Remove from heat and set aside.

In another skillet heat cooking oil. Combine flour and the ½ teaspoon salt. Toss chicken livers to coat. Sauté chicken livers in hot oil until golden brown on outside and pink inside, about 6 minutes. Drain livers well and combine with onion and mushrooms. Keep warm in chafing dish or fondue pot. Serve as appetizer with *toast*, or as entrée with hot *rice*. Makes 4 entrée servings.

Hint:
Kir is a good choice for a light party drink and is a favorite before-dinner drink of many Europeans. Make it by the glass using 1 tablespoon of crème de cassis, a sweet black currant liqueur, to 4 ounces of dry white wine. The proportions may vary, but the greater the proportion of liqueur, the sweeter the drink.

Appetizers

Whether your next party is formal or casual, large or small, a good assortment of appetizers is an essential beginning. Plan on variety — a dip to eat with vegetables — a spread or a molded mousse — and a bite-sized hors d'oeuvre. Make your choices from our selection of classic dips and hors d'oeuvres, and set the stage for a memorable affair.

SPICED COCKTAIL NUTS

- ¼ cup butter *or* margarine
- 1 tablespoon Worcestershire sauce
- ½ teaspoon bottled hot pepper sauce
- 1 tablespoon salad seasoning
- 1 teaspoon salt
- ½ teaspoon garlic salt
- ¼ teaspoon pepper
- 16 ounces shelled walnut halves *or* shelled whole almonds *or* shelled whole filberts

In 12-inch skillet with tight fitting lid combine butter or margarine, Worcestershire, hot pepper sauce, salad seasoning, salt, garlic salt, and pepper. Stir over low heat till blended. Add nuts, tossing to coat. Cook, covered, over low heat for 20 minutes, stirring occasionally. Cool on paper toweling. Store in airtight jar. Makes 4½ cups.

DILL SOUR CREAM DIP

- 1 cup dairy sour cream
- ½ cup mayonnaise
- 1 tablespoon finely chopped green onion
- 2 teaspoons dried parsley flakes, crushed
- 1 teaspoon dried dillweed
- 1 teaspoon seasoned salt
  Crackers or vegetable dippers

Combine sour cream, mayonnaise, green onion, parsley flakes, dillweed, and salt. Cover and chill several hours. Serve with crackers or vegetable dippers. Makes about 1½ cups.

SMOKED OYSTER DIP

    1 3-ounce package cream cheese, softened
    2 tablespoons mayonnaise
    2 tablespoons milk
    1 tablespoon finely chopped onion
    2 teaspoons chopped canned pimiento
    1 3⅔-ounce can smoked oysters, drained
       and chopped
       Assorted crackers or chips

Combine cream cheese, mayonnaise, milk,
onion, pimiento, and oysters; mix well. Chill.
Serve with crackers or chips. Makes 1 cup.

APPETIZER CHEESE MOUSSE

    2 teaspoons unflavored gelatin
    ¼ cup cold water
    2 cups dairy sour cream
    2 teaspoons Italian salad dressing mix
    ¼ cup crumbled blue cheese
    1 8-ounce carton (1 cup) small curd
       cream-style cottage cheese

Soften gelatin in cold water. Place over boiling
water and stir till gelatin dissolves. Stir gelatin
into sour cream; add Italian salad dressing mix,
blue cheese, and cottage cheese. Beat with
electric or rotary beater till well blended. Pour
into 3½-cup ring mold or small loaf pan. Chill till
firm; unmold and garnish. Serve with *crackers.*

GUACAMOLE

2 ripe medium avocados, peeled and pitted
2 tablespoons lemon juice
2 to 4 tablespoons chopped canned green
  chili peppers
1 thin slice of a small onion
1 clove garlic, crushed
⅛ teaspoon ground white pepper
½ teaspoon salt
  Crisp vegetable dippers *or* taco chips

In blender container combine avocados, lemon juice, chili peppers, onion slice, garlic, white pepper, and salt. Blend till smooth, scraping down sides of container as necessary. Serve as a dip with vegetables or taco chips. Makes 1 cup.

SHERRY WINE CHEESE SPREAD

4 cups shredded natural cheddar cheese
  (16 ounces)
½ cup crumbled blue cheese (2 ounces)
¼ cup butter *or* margarine, softened
½ cup dry sherry
2 teaspoons dry mustard
  Dash cayenne

In mixer bowl combine cheeses, butter or margarine, sherry, mustard, and cayenne. Beat till well blended. Pack into lightly oiled 1-cup molds or into one lightly oiled 3-cup mold. Cover tightly. Chill. Unmold and let stand at room temperature 1 hour before serving. Garnish with lettuce. Serve with *crackers* and *fruit*. Makes 3 cups.

CHEESE MEDLEY

1 cup shredded Swiss cheese (4 ounces)
1 cup shredded American cheese
  (4 ounces)
1 3-ounce package cream cheese, softened
¼ cup mayonnaise
2 tablespoons chopped pimiento
1 teaspoon Worcestershire sauce
½ teaspoon onion powder
¼ teaspoon bottled hot pepper sauce
½ cup crushed potato chips
1½ teaspoons grated Parmesan cheese

Bring Swiss cheese and American cheese to room temperature. In small mixing bowl beat together cream cheese and mayonnaise with electric mixer. Beat in Swiss and American cheeses. Add pimiento, Worcestershire, onion powder, and pepper sauce. Chill at least 1 hour. Shape into a ball. Mix potato chips and Parmesan cheese. Press over outside of ball. Wrap in clear plastic wrap. Refrigerate till firm. Makes 1 ball. Serve with *assorted crackers*.

CRAB-STUFFED MUSHROOMS

3 dozen large, whole, fresh mushrooms
1 7½-ounce can crab meat, drained,
  flaked, and cartilage removed
1 tablespoon snipped parsley
1 tablespoon chopped pimiento
1 teaspoon chopped capers
¼ teaspoon dry mustard
½ cup mayonnaise

Wash and dry mushrooms. With a sharp knife remove stems from mushrooms. (Save stems for use in another recipe.) Combine crab meat, parsley, pimiento, and capers. Blend dry mustard into mayonnaise; toss with crab mixture. Fill each mushroom crown with about 2 tablespoons crab mixture. Bake at 375° till hot, about 8 to 10 minutes. Makes 36 appetizers.

RESTAURANT INDEX

CALIFORNIA

Los Angeles, *Le Dôme,* 8720 Sunset Blvd., (213-659-6919). Recipe for *Clafoutis aux Cerises* on page 100.

Los Angeles, *Ma Maison,* 8368 Melrose Ave.,(Unlisted telephone).Recipe for *Lemon-Raspberry Tart* on page 103.

San Diego, *Star of the Sea Room,* 1360 Harbor Dr., (714-232-7408). Recipe for *Star of the Sea Salad* on page 96.

San Francisco, *Ernie's,* 847 Montgomery St., (415-397-5969). Recipe for *Chicken Cynthia à la Champagne* on page 116.

San Francisco, *Perry's,* 1944 Union St., (415-922-9022). Recipe for *Eggs Blackstone* on page 112.

San Francisco, *Washington Square Bar & Grill,* 1707 Powell St., (415-982-8123). Recipe for *The Vegetarian Joe* on page 120.

San Francisco, *Yamato,* 717 California at Grant, (415-397-3456). Recipe for *Tempura* on page 107.

DISTRICT OF COLUMBIA

Washington, *The Big Cheese,* 3139 M St. NW, (202-338-3314). Recipe for *Pohani Sir* on page 32.

Washington, *Csikós,* 3601 Connecticut Ave. NW, (202-362-5624). Recipe for *Rabbit Paprikas* on page 35.

FLORIDA

Miami, *Cafe Chauveron,* 9561 E. Bay Harbor Dr., (305-866-8779). Recipe for *Sole Véronique* on page 52.

Tampa, *Bern's Steak House,* 1208 S. Howard Ave., (813-251-2421). Recipe for *Brazilian Snow* on page 48.

GEORGIA

Roswell, *Gene and Gabe's Lodge*, 936 Canton St., (404-993-7588). Recipe for *Veal Bolognese* on page 44.

ILLINOIS

Chicago, *The Berghoff*, 17 W. Adams St., (312-427-3170). Recipe for *Ragout à la Deutsch* on page 80.

Chicago, *Gordon*, 512 N. Clark St., (312-467-9780). Recipe for *Kiwi and Strawberry Tart* on page 84.

KENTUCKY

Louisville, *Casa Grisanti*, 1000 E. Liberty St., (502-584-4377), Recipe for *Fettuccine con Pesto* on page 40.

LOUISIANA

New Orleans, *Brennan's*, 417 Royal St., (504-525-9711). Recipe for *Trout Kottwitz* on page 60.

New Orleans, *Jonathan*, 714 N. Rampart St., (504-586-1930). Recipe for *Oysters Thomas* on page 55.

MARYLAND

Baltimore, *Chesapeake Restaurant*, 1701 N. Charles St., (301-837-7711). Recipe for *Crab Imperial Chesapeake* on page 28.

MASSACHUSETTS

Boston, *Locke-Ober Café*, 3 and 4 Winter Pl., (617-542-1340). Recipe for *Breast of Chicken Sauté Richmond* on page 4.

MICHIGAN

Detroit, *London Chop House*, 155 W. Congress, (313-962-0277). Recipe for *Smoked Beef Omelet* on page 72.

Novi, *Ah Wok* 41563 W. 10 Mile Rd., (313-349-9260). Recipe for *Peanut Chicken* on page 75.

MINNESOTA

Minneapolis, *The New French Café*, 124 N. 4th St., (612-338-3790). Recipe for *Seviche à la Française* on page 92.

NEW YORK

New York City, *The Coach House*, 110 Waverly Place, (212-777-0303). Recipe for *Mushrooms à la Grecque* on page 16.

New York City, *The Palm*, 837 Second Ave., (212-697-2953). Recipe for *Steak à la Stone* on page 20.

New York City, *The Russian Tea Room*, 150 W. 57th St., (212-757-4182). Recipe for *Shashlik Caucasian* on page 12.

New York City, *Windows on the World*, 107th Floor, One World Trade Center, (212-938-1111). Recipe for *Frozen Soufflé Amaretto* on page 8.

OREGON

Portland, *Nendel's*, 9900 SW Canyon Rd., (503-297-2551). Recipe for *Chicken Livers Sautéed* on page 128.

PENNSYLVANIA

Philadelphia, *Frog*, 264 S. 16th St., (215-735-8882). Recipe for *Thai Chicken Curry* on page 24.

TEXAS

Dallas, *Bagatelle*, 4925 Greenville at University, (214-692-8224). Recipe for *Roast Duck à la Normande* on page 67.

Dallas, *Ewald's*, 5415 W. Lovers Ln., (214-357-1622). Recipe for *Shrimp du Chef* on page 64.

WASHINGTON

Seattle, *The Golden Lion*, The Olympic Hotel, Fifth at University, (206-682-7700). Recipe for *Celery Victor* on page 123.

WISCONSIN

Milwaukee, *Mader's*, 1041 N. Third St., (414-271-3377). Recipe for *Black Forest Cherry Torte* on page 87.

RECIPE INDEX

Le Nouveau Cafe Français

LODGE

AHWDK

Mader's

LOCKE-OBER CAFÉ
EST 1875
WINTER PLACE

Ma Paison

Csikós

Washington Square
Bar & Grill.

NENDEL'S

london chop house.

Brennan's

Cafe Chauveron

The Russian Tea Room

BERN'S St

LE
DOME

Ewald's

Chesapeake Restaurant

WINDOWS O

Bag

The Berghoff

Frog

Star
Ro

ERNIE'S

The BIG CHEESE

THE PALM

Perry's

Casa Gri

Ma Paison

Go

london chop house.

BERN'S STEAK HOUSE

NEW ORLEANS
JONATHAN
A RESTAURANT

gene & gabe's

LODGE

WINDOWS ON THE WORLD

THE NEW FRENCH CAFE
Le Nouveau Cafe Français

LOCKE-OBER CAFÉ
EST 1875
WINTER PLACE

Bagatelle

Star of the Sea
Room

Mader's

Washington Square
Bar & Grill.

NEN

THE
COACH·HOUSE

Brennan's

Cafe C

Casa Grisanti

✿ **yamato**

The Russian Tea Room

GORDON

LE
DOME

The Golden Lion

Chesape